YOU SANG IT BACK TO ME

AMANDA DEO

MAD RUSH BOOKS

You Sang It Back to Me
Amanda Deo

ISBN 978-1-304-32446-7
Published by Lulu.com

Cover by Ryan W. Bradley
Interior layout by Craig Scott

Pieces included in this work have previously been published in *Apt, Literary Orphans, Gobbet, Short, Fast and Deadly, Negative Suck, Ditch, Word Riot,* and *1/25.*

The accompanying playlist for the third part of this collection can be found at http://bit.ly/adeosongs.

Mad Rush Books
http://1of25.tumblr.com

Many thanks owed to all the editors for taking the time to make me feel pretty *kick ass* and to C.S. for taking a chance on me. Thank you to R.W.B. for providing me with endless sweet graphics.

you couldn't call or come to me
i sang it out, you sang it back to me
you sang it back to me, sang it back to me
you sang it back to me

"Promise of the West"
The Jealous Sound

I. *i'm sorry i'm leaving*
II. *in a city*
III. *you sang it back to me*

i'm sorry i'm leaving

IN A DREAM YOU MELTED

You go to work. The clothes you pick out are hanging on the back of the chair in the living room. On a different day I close my eyes and the clothes are gone and your body is thin air. I'm making breakfast for me and him and we have a little boy but I'm not his mother. And somewhere you've evaporated. Somewhere you are making another girl a cup of tea.

IF IT WERE AN ACCIDENT I WOULD FORGIVE YOU

We're talking about poets & you don't know any of them. We keep having the same dream. The dream where I'm in two places at once & you are trying to piece together my choices & four feet & two hesitant mouths.

At a diner in New Jersey I tell you that everything is just so big. That *everything I know hurts me more than it hurts you.*

BECAUSE YOU DON'T HAVE ANYONE

We hit a fox the night after you get arrested. The headlights are wet with *SHIT HAPPENS.* You catch my shaking hands from shattering your teeth. From giving myself another black eye. I cradle the fox and hold her like four years of it won't happen again.

I strap her into the car seat and you drive away, drive away, drive away.

ELECTRONS

In the middle of winter you sell me patience and I talk and you laugh. You weren't broke you were what I spent on heaven and electrons. The centre of our bodies is nothing to brag about. There's a spark at breakfast and by dinner no one gives a shit about the cold.

I'm so tired of donations and opposites and *she comes first.*

BLOOD SUGAR

The biggest mistake is the future. If I knew how to ask we wouldn't be here. You can't take back what you said when there was room for expansion. The end of the world comes at the end of a word with less girls to hit on. You were a rough draft and basketball practice. I wouldn't be caught dead without you.

COMET

I started you out of boredom. We eat different landscapes in front of the tv. When I take off my shirt, you take off your shirt. Your muscle always stays inside the guts of eventually we fuck up and turn back and get lost. You are what I saw when I booked the clouds.

When are you coming out?

We should probably talk soon.

LIONHEART

Your growl is arm's length. On a drive to your house we pick up magazines and cigarettes. A set of hives holds me closer. A view of the lake is all we've ever wanted inside my head. There is no connection between I let it slip and four legs and we can't still. I twist my hair until she disappears.

HARVEY DENT

I fuck for less than parking tickets and more than love notes. I do what I can to hold up the universe. I've placed my coin in your lap, on top of your coffee cup.

There's nothing between my ears and everything between my legs.

My right side said **YES** on the first date.

DIVINE EROS

I drink the funeral in a dream. I give satisfaction in voice overs. In an instant. I hold attention with it's better than a lie and your eyebrows are so pretty and it wasn't only once. Every pew has a set of broken legs and a last breath and an obvious confession.

Your jeans sag to the right. Your briefcase sits next to the door. I'm never yours.

WE HAPPEN HERE

In the bathroom at the lodge. A smile wrapped around my ankles. I've got a new name for everything. You were never the someone I recognized. **You were never the harvest I thought you were**.

NIGHT OUT

I was a city. A strobe light hits your face and dies and her. A slice of rust is what keeps us apart. The only thing I can do is approve.

GAP

You are full of missing. The gap between your front teeth was never enough. I want you to know that I know *I don't need this shit.* I'm somewhere waiting for a softer body.

IN A CITY

I'm the temperature of your bones. You piss designs in the snow. I will meet you there. I'm sorry we came.

THE KICK OFF

I'm not sure what you will look like when you die.

I curse.

I drag my suitcase towards the front door with all the crap my mom gave me.

People have sex on the internet all the time, I say.

AT THE WEDDING

I wear a white dress.

I vomit on hers.

I fuck with the band. I yell at them to play Sublime. I skank my ass off. I'm the only one on the dance floor.

I punch her dad; *he's a pussy.*

I thank everyone for coming.

I spit on my sister's dress and rub out the throw-up with my underwear.

PANDORA

These are the
things you've
never seen.

Tell me how I
keep it
this way.

WE WOKE UP LEAN

I smoke gently on your chest. We were careful not to wake the kids & goodbye with a handshake & my skeleton is trapped with your universe inside. I grew up in the living room & hatched during the delivery of us but no one cared.

Your heart sounds like spokes.

Isn't breaking.

Not at all.

IN THE WILD

He forecasts more tornadoes. He forecasts them all year. In the eye of the storm we sit on lawn chairs and he thinks about forgiving me. I hate myself in the wild.

But this is how I operate, I say.

This is how I love and control.

in a city
(for JD)

BUFFALO, NY

I can't sing the
blues. It's

been 16 hours.

I'm starting to
think I'm awesome
without you.

NEW YORK, NY

Used car lot.
Used car lot.
Used car lot.

You.

ROSELLE PARK, NJ

I see you across the room. I don't want to know what you're wearing.

You arranged the suitcases in our closet so yours was on top. So yours was out first.

I forgot what it was like to stay bright.

NIAGARA FALLS, ON

I'm pulling at
your split
ends.

When you
see the Falls
you can't stop
staring &

I know I've
lost you.

TORONTO, ON

It's like a temporary tattoo, he says.

Like the ones they give out at baseball games and county fairs and Hindu weddings.

I scrub it for a week, a month, five years.

The top of Rosedale deep inside my chest.

Pack my bags.

MONTREAL, QC

I said it's
where poets
go to die and
where we play
air guitar at
their funerals.

When you
lean a little
to the left
I don't want
to be here
anymore.

CRANFORD, NJ

We split spoons
when we
met.

Oh God I
need you.

I take out
my hair pins.

ASPEN, CO

I'll spend this much to love you. I can't hear the mountains in hot tubs. I put an accent on every part of your body. I found out that the ground is our heaviest memory. I've been re-writing this under pylons and paint cans and backlogs. **I've been advised that you're not anything**.

MANCHESTER, UK

A walk. I've kenneled your memories numbers one through twenty-two. The lottery I never won.

CORKTOWN, TO

It was the day when we were all coming up & you were going down & you were giving me advice on how **this is & is not success**.

When you pretend to miss me I walk by the market and forget to be brave. The only thing I'm doing tonight is swallowing the hairs off your pillow and looking for a reason to hide our heavy bodies.

I just want you to be useful.

PRINCETON, NJ

Someone is dying on a collegiate lawn somewhere. I hear the kids are super fresh and sing power ballads in preppy bars. I'm waiting on a text and the tv won't turn on and the electric is off and this is not what I thought it would be. Behind the Buffy poster on your wall is where I left all my good years. You said you ran out of gas. You said we were lost.

MONTCLAIR, NJ

Let me see what shape your nails are in. It's too late to say ever. I love you in ways that don't exist or no one cares about or a piano can't play. I'm not sure if I can keep it up. Everything we have said translates into *I'm not sure where you are.*

TWEED, ON

You don't owe me anything. I ride the elevator at work and wish I kissed your best friend. You tap the side of a hat and pull your words out. Who could forget ***Sweet Caroline*** and when your mother had a stroke and this bus is everything and nothing

you sang it back to me
(for PK)

BEST FRIENDS
(for Ruben and Rachel)

I'm in way over my head.

I say, I don't understand why you don't get my jokes.

You reply that you don't get them because *we've never fucked.*

"Soco Amaretto Lime"
Brand New

SWEET HAIRCUTS RULE

I fixate on the small, perfect hairs aligned on your scalp and finger bang myself to sleep. In my head I haze you as part of your initiation to be in my body. There's a puddle of ceiling that seeps through a mattress & leaks into a possibility & thank God we're still young. My hands arch intensely to an ex's mixed cd.

I profess that this never happened. Temporarily happened. I heard that falling birds sometimes do this & fall into a lap they aren't supposed to.

"Set Yourself on Fire"
Stars

IT HAPPENED ON A WEEKEND

We've got one more day, he says.

There's a half-eaten sandwich in
the rearview mirror.

A finger missing a
ring.

Here comes a
city.

"Stationary, Stationary"
Anberlin

GOLD RUSH

And then you left for the West. You told me the tar sands don't wait for anyone and especially not the father of two little kids. I knew you were made of panic and broken sleep and laid off.

When you called me from a new number you shook like burning coal and you cracked tired and aching. There was a smoke ring around your guilt so big an Inuit curled up and slept inside. A nightlight grasped our loneliness.

We were spoiled and whispering and we were grateful for it.

"But All the Regrets Are Killing Me"
American Football

A DAY WHEN WE WERE CELEBRATING

I thought about you when we got to the place. I tried to act like I had never been there before. The smell reminded me of the escarpment and the greenbelt I unfastened from your waste. An emergency in a wallet. *Still wrapped.*

"No One Really Wins"
Copeland

HAPPY SATURDAY NIGHT LOVERS FROM ST. KITTS

At midnight I cup you into the moonlight of an Ikea mattress. I fall asleep and wake up and fall asleep and we both survive. I tell you that ten years ago I had a heart attack that moved up from a punk band and down into the souls of my feet and I text and pace.

And St. Kitts squeezed my lungs all the way to Buffalo behind a hauler carrying cedar shakes. We both say it was different back then. It all came so much sooner than I thought it would.

"A Dozen Roses"
Braid

THE DAY YOU BECAME A FATHER

I pillow talk & sit in the back of your truck & my every thrill is bitten back by baby teeth. I don't know what you mean to her & I don't know how to conquer you in this state. The day you became a father I couldn't get wet. I barely had room to say *I'M SORRY*. All my drunk dials were put on hold.

Sometimes I almost forget they're there.

Sometimes I whisper *bastard* under my breath.

"The Funeral"
Band of Horses

RESERVES

You're in the driveway and you don't want to see her. At university I wrote you in margins so I would have proof. I wait for a moment when the upstairs curtain is pulled back and no one cares enough and she looks away and turn off your headlights. I've been wrong about every genie. Each one of them has talked me into *anywhere for anything for anyone.*

I'm pretty sure it's just the same thing we say over and over again even if it feels different.

IN CASE HE DIES OR
LEAVES ME
OR STAYS

"A Long Night My Love"
Cuff the Duke

FULL NEST

I google the possibility of making a tiny grave. If I time it right I will be on hold for just a little longer. Every time I look at you there are two dumb mouths that slip between stretch marks. There is a gap between leaving me in a hotel parking lot & I care about you & photo-stalking is an apology.

“We Can Have It”
The Dears

WE'RE GROWING OUT

On another day you decide it's best to leave. He wears a Spider-Man costume to the mall and you pass all the hot moms while you hold his hand and a scream carries all the way to the back of Sears. But it's not his, ***it's yours***. Everything you need to leave behind is important. Your kids, your house, the birds, an argument about a lost job, furniture that holds you, but the thought of forgetting she's your computer password thrills you.

You pass the hot moms again.

Nothing to see here, he says, through a hole you slit so he could breathe.

You didn't even know he could talk.

"To Be Alone With You"
Sufjan Stevens

PARTY HAT

She would wonder how I could take care of them because I'd never been a mother. She had a point. The strap from a party hat rubbed against my chin so I took it off. She was seven and I bought her makeup and her mother called me a *slut* without calling me a *slut.*

I watched her tiny eyes looking at him. And I watched how he looked at me and how I looked back at her and I knew we would be okay.

"Icarus"
White Hinterland

I'M NOT SURE HOW TO PLAY SECOND

She asked me to buy her skates but I wasn't sure. I couldn't connect our pasts and felt guilty sharing me with her. She showed me a baby photo of her first bath. In the kitchen sink their hands touched and they had small, kitten grins on their faces.

We'll get you the skates next year, I say.

"In the Water, I am Beautiful"
City and Colour

SLEEPOVER

The first time he brought her to my house was for a sleepover. I didn't think it was appropriate but I didn't want to question him; *he was the parent.* Plus, I wanted him in my bed without having to hide it from her. The boy stayed with the mother. I let her watch *Dirty Dancing* but I kept the liquor cabinet locked for both of us. When it was time for her to go to bed she asked him to sleep with her in the living room, so I slept alone.

"Acrobat"
As Tall As Lions

HOW DO YOU KNOW YOU'RE READY

He wanted me to become good at co-parenting. I knew this would be hard for me so I called a friend for advice.

Remember that time, she said, *that you gave an underage kid a hand job on the dance floor?*

We laughed so hard I cried.

He told me not to come over.

"William and Betsy"
The Winston Jazz Routine

HABS AND LEAFS

People think we don't take these things seriously, but we do. The night you got married the Habs played the Leafs. Or maybe I was playing you, *I'm not really sure*. I watched YouTube videos about the best car crashes of all time. When I closed my eyes I felt each impact. There are people out there who say they would die for you but I'm not confident they would if given the chance. You invited me to the wedding but I didn't go. I knew there was a flower girl standing in between the night you told me you loved me and the night I told you it wouldn't work.

"Decisions, Decisions"
The Starting Line

A FRAME

We went to a lot of bars. We were comfortable there. Before you left you texted me a picture of your boy eating cereal off the floor with his hands. I could see the back of her shoe in the corner of the picture and I knew it would be the kind of photo you would send to your mother. An hour later you phoned to let me know he was sick and dizzy and needed you. I still went to the bar. I knew the picture wasn't meant for me any way.

"The Heart is a Lonely Hunter"
The Anniversary

SECOND STRING

The kids were getting ready for Halloween and you asked if I wanted to help carve pumpkins. The small ones hugged each other and danced around to "Monster Mash" as I held onto your happiness. I thought, *I'm adjusting. I can do this.* I let her hold the small carving knife and she cut herself in the down loop of a jagged mouth. She screamed and you were angry but you also felt sorry for me so I cut myself with the knife and started screaming too. She asked for the phone. She asked for the mother.

"The Sea is a Good Place to Think About
the Future"
Los Campesinos!

PACKED LUNCH

She wrote a letter addressed to you and the mother. She said she loved you for being so kind and she loved you for making her food. The mother went on a holiday abroad and left you with the kids. I thought it was big of me to step in and help out where I could and fuck you while they were at school. I thought it best not to remind you that they weren't mine. It was anything but a dream come true. I forced your hand to my stomach and hummed. You walked away to take a shower without saying anything.

She came home with the lunches, still packed and untouched, all week.

"Guns of Memorial Park"
Sparta

PREGNANCY PACT

I got a place over there and a new job. You stayed with me on the weekends to avoid splitting hairs. I'm not sure what the mother knew but I didn't care and I never asked. When you came in the door I pretended to cook dinner. I slung my arms around your neck and pushed them back into their mother's body. I rode them back into the nights they happened until I came so loud they never existed. When I found out I was pregnant we drove to the closest bar and got drunk.

It could be worse, I said. *You could be losing me instead.*

"The Futile"
Say Anything

FIVE DEAL BREAKERS FOR DATING A DAD

i.

Sunday morning brought me two kids. I was still hung-over from the night before. I stumbled into the living room with eyeliner across my thighs and a phone number scribbled on my forearm in cologne that I was trying to hide. They were perfect little beings with little backpacks and real mouths. You lovingly pushed them onto the couch red faced and embarrassed. I offered milk, *bad.* Juice, *out.* I laughed but I didn't mean it. I collected the mail, some of it months old. *How do I throw out all of this junk?*

ii.

We had dinner plans. I bought a new dress and straightened my hair. I looked fucking hot. I put on my favourite underwear hoping they'd come off before we got out the door. I took them off to be covered in you. To save time. Because I hadn't seen you all week. Because the mother said she'd have the kids. Because I could finally pin your wings down. Because they were in a school play and your daughter cried when you said you couldn't go. Because I sat home in my underwear on the corner of the couch instead.

iii.

I showed her the new room. It was pink but she liked purple. *Pink is for little girls. Pink was the colour of her room before she was born. There is so much you don't know.* I closed my eyes. I was sorry. I kept on wanting a different outcome.

iv.

He had swallowed a small bone. I cooked chicken breast for dinner. As far as I knew, the mother made ready-meals most of the time and I wanted to show them how different I was. I wanted to one-up her. I noticed your hard-on and rested my legs freely on your lap when we sat down to eat. As he choked I was confused and rational and needed a minute or two to think it through. *How was this possible?* As you squeezed his tiny chest my heart exploded and when the bone was free, she asked for French fries.

V.

You want to let me down easy. You say you fell in love with me before they came along and you can't mirror us all up. I'm not in the puzzle and I'm fucked. *We're broken animals,* you say. You keep on saying *Before them.*

Before them.
Before them.
Before them.

Before them I was the girl of your dreams.

"Plath Heart"
Braids

YOUR DAD IS A REALLY NICE GUY

Your dad is a really nice guy and he thinks I'm really pretty and he hates me. He can *see* why you left the mother but he doesn't *know* why. He sees me juggle the kids. He watches me fail at PTA and a purse full of Band-Aids, cough syrup and inhalers. He knows I don't have a clue but you don't know because I'm everything you've ever wanted and he hates it. I attempt to draw them close underneath a single umbrella as we leave your parents' house. Your daughter's hair is soaking wet. He watches me from the window with a broken heart.

"The Recluse"
Cursive

YOU SANG IT BACK TO ME

You brush her hair. She winks at you as you rub her back. When she's sick she slips into your bed and fake coughs and gives you a Swiss army knife for Father's Day. You take her to opening day and don't tell the mother.

You let her crack and break and forgive.

When you sing it back to me I can't fold up the words and I can't swallow them until they become forever.

A baby. A shotgun wedding. **A future we don't want to know**.

"Promise of the West"
The Jealous Sound

AMANDA DEO is the author of *North of the Mason-Dixon Line* (In/Words, 2005). She is an audiophile. She lives in Toronto with her husband and a chubby beagle.

ALSO FROM MAD RUSH BOOKS

Magazines
1/25
Mad Rush

Collections
God's Will by Scott Urban
Open Hand Falling by Craig Scott
Jupiter Orgasma by Catfish McDaris
Waiting on Nothing by Catfish McDaris
Punk Me by Patricia Hickerson
Tales From a French Envelope by Catfish McDaris & Craig Scott

http://1of25.tumblr.com
http://www.lulu.com/spotlight/madrush

www.ingramcontent.com/pod-product-compliance
Ingram Content Group UK Ltd.
Pitfield, Milton Keynes, MK11 3LW, UK
UKHW020218250726
13967UKWH00001B/70